AMERICA

AMERICA

PHOTOGRAPHS BY JAKE RAJS

FOREWORD BY JAMES A. MICHENER

UNIVERSE

Pages 2–3: Farmland, Idaho

Page 4: Byers Lake and Mt. McKinley, Denali National Park, Alaska

Pages 6–7: San Francisco, California

Pages 10–11: Magnolia Gardens, South Carolina

Page 12: Space Shuttle *Discovery*, John F. Kennedy Space Center, Cape Canaveral, Florida

Pages 14–15: Acoma Pueblo, New Mexico

Paperback edition (abridged)
Published in the United States of America in 1996 by
  UNIVERSE PUBLISHING
A Division of Rizzoli International Publications, Inc.
  300 Park Avenue South
  New York, NY 10010

Clothbound edition first published in the United States of America in 1990 by Rizzoli International Publications, Inc.

Library of Congress catalog card number: 95-61918
    98 99 00 / 10 9 8 7 6 5 4 3 2

Design by Gilda Hannah
Printed in Italy

To my father
whose vision of freedom
brought me to America

CONTENTS

OUR AMERICA

This book is a joyous celebration! Its sparkling photographs remind us of the extraordinary land our nation occupies, and a review of them shows us how fortunate we are to live where we do.

Our nation is a mansion erected on three powerful pillars: the creative mix of our citizenry; the moral, political, and economic principles which it built; and, basic to all else, the glorious land we have been able to occupy.

A principal fact about that land is its continental dimension, stretching as it does clear across North America, from the Atlantic to the Pacific. Most nations do not have the freedom of movement which comes from such magnitude. From birth we Americans are accustomed to hugeness of scale. We are not pinned down in a corner. We are free to range across an entire continent, taking our children where we will. And those children are free to construct their lives anywhere from Maine to California, from Oregon to Florida.

This bigness provides us with a spacious landscape in which to experiment, at times achieving wonders that would not be possible in a cramped area, at other times making colossal mistakes, as in our farming programs, yet always able to survive and bounce back, partly because we are so large that we can absorb bad knocks.

Our land is not only spacious, it is also unbelievably rich: coal in the east, iron ore in the north, gold in the west, oil in the southwest, trees everywhere, fields so vast and fertile they could feed most of the world, and copious supplies of water to nourish them.

I have sometimes thought that the significant difference between Australia and the United States can be explained only by the differing gifts of nature.

The two countries are of comparable size, Australia at just under three million square miles, the United States somewhat above three and a half. But Australia, on her relatively deprived land can support only fifteen million people, while the United States can provide for more than two hundred and forty million. A principal reason for this vast difference is that down the middle of our nation flows the sovereign Mississippi River with its major tributaries: the far-reaching Missouri, the powerful Ohio, the quiet Tennessee, the wandering Arkansas, plus their networks: the Yellowstone, the Platte, Allegheny, Kentucky, Red. Rip that intricate river system from the heartland of our nation, and the states lying inland from the Atlantic and Pacific Oceans would be the Great American Desert. Like Australia, we would be able to support only a small population clinging to our two seacoasts, and numbering not in the hundreds of millions but in the tens. And with such limited numbers, the empty areas would not be able to supply markets for the industries of our coastal cities and manufacturing districts. We should be grateful that we are a big land, with adequate water, at least for the present.

Therefore I am glad to see among these handsome pictures a reminder of our almost limitless grain fields (93, South Dakota), our magnificent woodlands (52, California), our soaring mountains (64, Oregon), and our life-giving rivers (104–105, Minnesota). They remind us of our good fortune.

There are other corners of the earth comparably blessed by nature on which great civilizations have not arisen, and I believe the difference lies in the kinds of people who occupied our land.

America had the good fortune to be settled by people—those already here at the beginning and those who arrived later—who were sturdy, strong-minded, courageous, and determined to preserve the riches and the freedom they found here.

It required tremendous heroism for our original Indians to leave their natal Siberia some forty thousand years ago, cross the Bering Ice Bridge then exposed, and wander down onto what would later become western America. There they multiplied, making the land and its natural features—rivers, lakes, and buffalo—their own.

The first Europeans who arrived to share the land with them were a determined people: the rebellious English who placed their stamp upon the new nation; the daring French who in the earliest years explored where the English seemed afraid to venture; the sturdy, well-educated Germans; and then, starting in the 1820s, that constant inflow of Europeans who rushed here to escape economic, social and military tyranny, that flood of patriots from Austria, Scandinavia, Russia, Poland, Italy, and the Slavic states. We gathered jewels from the far corners of the earth.

Then came the industrious settlers from Asia: the Chinese, the Japanese, the Filipinos with their manifold skills. In my own lifetime, I have been involved intimately with new floods of settlers who have come here to seek our time-honored freedoms: the excellent Hungarians in 1956, the powerfully oriented Cubans in the 1960s, the Vietnamese of the 1970s. What a powerful mix of people!

Of major significance in our national life, always present, always contributing, were the Africans who arrived in slavery and fought their way to equality. They form a constant thread in our history, a noble one that gives our nation a distinctive quality.

Had this flood of settlers arrived in America barren of ideas, I doubt they could have accomplished much, even though they inherited a paradise. Fortunately, they reached our shores exploding with ideas, with moral convictions, with inventive concepts, and with the courage to fight for what they believed. It was from this cauldron of seething convictions that our nation emerged.

The earliest settlers knew precisely what they wanted: freedom of religion, freedom to trade in new patterns, freedom to educate their children, freedom to move about, and freedom from royal absolutism. Thus motivated, they erected here societies which enabled them to achieve the goals denied them at home. We were fortunate to have started our nation with such morally rigorous people, for their solid ideas would give direction to all that followed.

The people who started our nation believed in God, the prudence of Bible teaching, the right of each man to worship as he saw fit. The convictions became so engrained in our national conscience that, when our founding fathers launched their Revolution in 1776, they sought divine guidance in their struggle against oppression. We are a nation brought into being by men and women of faith, and the simple Vermont church shown on page 103 bespeaks their rugged beliefs. The more ornate steeples which dominate the Maine village on page 126 represent church buildings across the land.

But the men who framed our Constitution had witnessed so much religious dictatorship and even persecution in their study of history, in both Europe and their own colonies, that they repeatedly refused in their Convention in Philadelphia in 1787 to allow any church-state relationship. Despite Benjamin Franklin's almost tearful plea that the delegates declare their work to have been done under divine guidance, they would not do so. In fact, they even refused to discuss the matter. Organized religion is not mentioned in the original Constitution, and the first provision of the later Bill of Rights is a caution against allowing the new Republic to establish a state religion, or to abridge such freedom of religion as already existed in the colonies. The men who established our nation wanted us to be a moral nation but not doctrinaire, and we have been determined to remain so.

From the beginning, the character of our country has expressed itself in its social traditions: a wide variety of free churches, free-speaking newspapers, free public education, public roads and waterways, transportation probing into the remotest corners of the land, colleges, libraries, hospitals, museums, theaters, orchestras, local and national parks, plus a profusion of clubs like Boy and Girl Scouts for children, Rotary and Daughters of the American Revolution for grown-ups, Parent-Teacher Associations, support groups for local hospitals, the American Legion, labor unions, alumni who collect funds to support their universities, those worthy groups who protect defenseless children and animals, and the excited citizens who support the political candidates of their choice or initiate and try to pass referendums.

No stranger could hope to understand the United States, unless she or he followed the contributions of the constructive groups. They are voluntary. Their members work without pay, and they are inspired by the highest principles of our national heritage. When I travel abroad, and see some heinous social injustice, I am apt to cry: "That would never be allowed in the United States!" by which I probably mean: "The good women of our town would not permit a condition like that to continue." And then I add: "Their busy husbands might ignore it, but their wives would press the issue." I am enormously proud of what the women of America have pressured their husbands to do.

A salvation of our country has been its ability to conduct a vigorous and at times almost violent political life—go to the polls on Tuesday, cast our vote, and on Wednesday morning say calmly: "All right! This time the other side won. Let them rule for four years, and then we'll take another crack at them." This commendable willingness to join forces the morning after a heated election is in stark contrast to the political behavior of many European and Asian nations in which the voting takes place on Sunday, but the real election begins next day when no clear-cut mandate has been delivered, and the various minority parties launch a three-week hassle to determine what coalition of disparate parties will govern, tenuously.

And our system of conferring immediate responsibility on the winning team is infinitely superior to the Latin American one of installing a civilian president, but then encouraging the military to throw him out and establish their own petty dictatorship. Orderly politics is the mark of a mature nation, and we are twice fortunate that our predecessors got us started right, and that we have preserved their admirable system.

In recent decades the economic life of any nation has assumed such dominating importance that many Americans have come to believe that the most valuable asset in our life is our system of semi-regulated capitalism. It seems to provide maximum welfare for the maximum number of people, and it has been the success of this system, in the United States and in the other democracies, that has revealed Communism to be such a deficient alternative. The older I grow the more respect I have for our American system, but I have certainly seen times when even it faltered. As a young man in the Great Depression, I witnessed so many things which needed correction that I might have become an extreme socialist, but I refrained because I believed that we had, as a people, the brains to make corrections. We did, and I lived to see many of the injustices which had worried me removed.

I have remained sensitive to social and economic injustice and today see many spots on our national fabric that cry out for cleaning up: a more stable money system; a reduced debt; a return to a goods-producing economy rather than a consuming one; greater productivity in our work force; wiser management at the top; the elimination of laws which allow and encourage any financial wizard to use junk securities to gain control of major producing companies, gut them for quick personal profit, then throw thousands of working men and women out of the jobs they had expected to last their lifetimes.

Two problems seem to supersede all others: the insidious terror of drugs and the growing gap between rich and poor, illustrated by the fact that even young people of good character and work habits cannot afford to own homes for their families, while many at the bottom of the social order can find no homes at all and must live on the streets. We should dedicate ourselves to the eradication of such impediments.

These exquisite photographs remind us of how precious our heritage is. The grandeur of our landscape is revealed in shots like those of the Grand Canyon (70–71, Arizona), Mt. McKinley (4, Alaska), and Sankaty Light (115, Massachusetts).

The appropriateness of how our ancestors built on their land is shown in the architectural simplicity of the rural farm (72–73, Vermont) and the stately grace of the plantation (96–97, Louisiana). While their plans for expansion and development are recognized in our great cities of today: San Francisco, Washington, DC, Houston, and New York (148–149, 181, 146–147, 188–189).

The people who wander through these pages add color to their land: the lonely pool shooter (85, Arkansas), the taro farmer (94–95, Hawaii) and, best of all, the Navajo father forming an ideal cradle for his son (84, Arizona). I was fascinated by the shot of the Indianapolis speedway (169), because I could not figure out in which direction the two cars headed. Then it became clear. The top car has gone into a tire-burning spin, has made a hundred-and-eighty degree whirl, and is headed for disaster.

Because I cherish the animals who share America with me, I was delighted to see portraits of creatures about which I have written: the bald eagle of Alaska (53), and the buffalo of South Dakota (66-67).

Repeated study of these photographs ought to instill in each of us a determination to leave our land in at least as good condition as when we received it...or better.

James A. Michener
Texas Center for Writers
Austin, Texas

In Wildness is the preservation of the world.

—*Henry David Thoreau*

WILDERNESS

Page 31: Waterfall, Hawaii, Hawaii

Page 32: Buffalo, Theodore Roosevelt National Park, North Dakota

Page 33: Wild horses, Theodore Roosevelt National Park, North Dakota

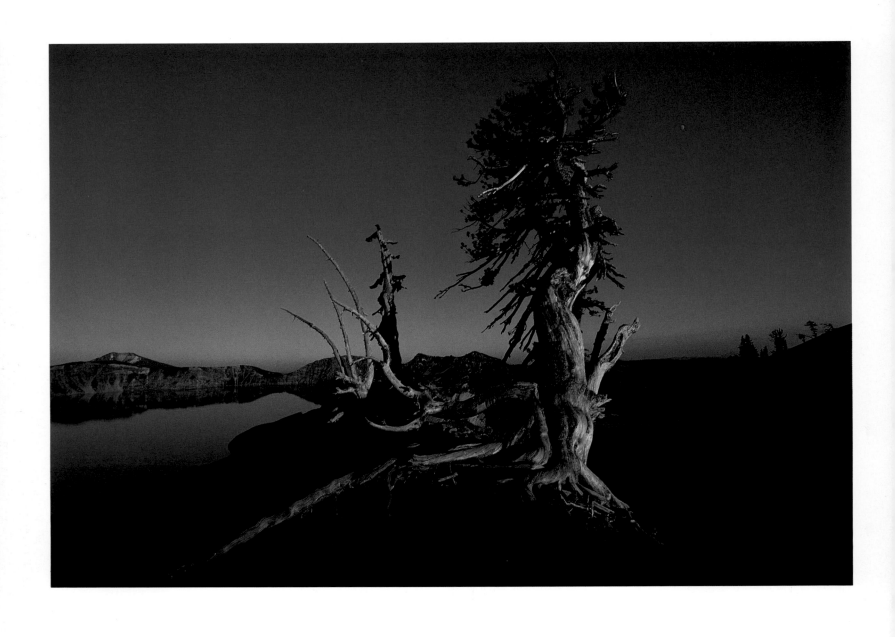

Pages 34–35: Crater Lake National Park, Oregon

Page 36: White Sands National Monument, New Mexico

Page 37: Potomac River, Arlington, Virginia

Page 39: Lake Powell, Gunsight Canyon, Glen Canyon
National Recreation Area, Utah/Arizona

Pages 40–41: Fall reflection, New Hampshire

Page 42 (above): Red Rock Canyon, Las Vegas area, Nevada

Page 42 (below): Bryce Canyon National Park, Utah

Page 43: Zion National Park, Utah

Page 45: White House Ruin, Canyon de Chelly National Monument, Arizona

Page 47: Moose, Wonder Lake, Denali National Park, Alaska

Pages 48–49: Blue heron, Okefenokee National Wildlife Refuge, Georgia

Pages 50–51: Wildflowers, Brenham, Texas

Page 52: Jedediah Smith Redwoods State Park, California

Page 53 (above): Bald eagle, Haines, Alaska

Page 53 (below): Hoh Rain Forest, Olympic National Park, Washington

Pages 54–55: The Windows, Arches National Park, Utah

Page 63 (above): Snow geese, Bombay Hook National Wildlife Refuge, Delaware

Page 63 (below): Tundra swans, Lake Mattamuskeet, North Carolina

Page 64 (above): Mt. Hood and Lost Lake, Oregon

Page 64 (below): Lake Sherburne, Glacier National Park, Montana

Page 65 (above): Mt. Whitney, California

Page 65 (below): Snake River, Grand Teton National Park, Wyoming

Pages 66–67: Buffalo, Badlands National Park, South Dakota

Page 69: Sand and butte, Monument Valley, Navajo Nation, Arizona/Utah

Pages 70–71: Grand Canyon, Arizona

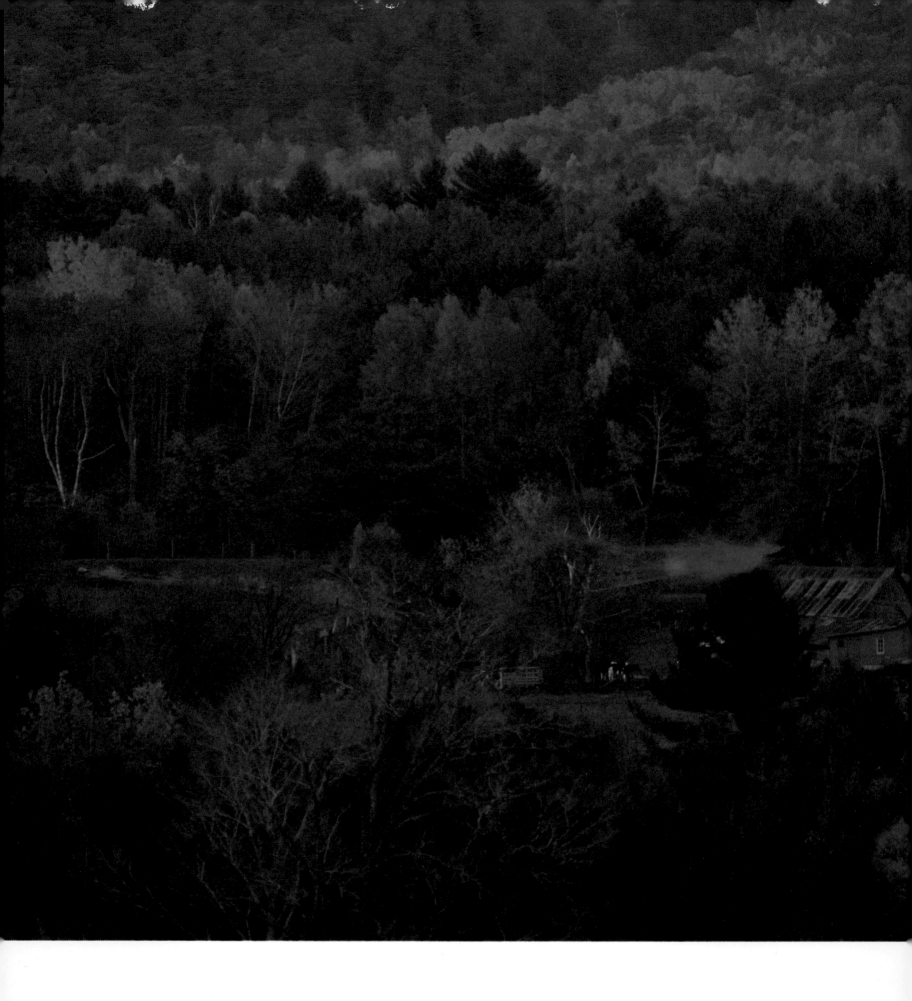

The farmers . . . are the founders of human civilization.

—*Daniel Webster*

FARMS AND TOWNS

Page 80: National Fresh Water Fishing Hall of Fame, Hayward, Wisconsin

Page 81: Mountain View, Arkansas

Pages 82–83: Flower farm, near Gilroy, California

Page 84: Father and child, Kayenta, Navajo Nation, Arizona

Page 85: Busters Recreation Hall, Mountain View, Arkansas

Pages 86–87: Farm, near Dover, Delaware

The river is within us, the sea is all about us;

The sea is the land's edge also, the granite

Into which it reaches, the beaches where it tosses

Its hints of earlier and other creation.

—T. S. Eliot

SHORELINES

Afoot and lighthearted I take to the open road,

Healthy, free, the world before me,

The long brown path before me leading wherever I choose . . .

Strong and content, I travel the open road.

—Walt Whitman

ROADWAYS

Far below and around lay the city like a ragged purple dream,
the wonderful, cruel, enchanting, bewildering, fatal, great city.

—O. Henry

CITIES

Page 154: Construction worker, Union, New Jersey

Page 155: Gateway Arch, St. Louis, Missouri

Page 156: Mission San Xavier del Bac, also called White Dove
of the Desert, Tucson, Arizona

Page 157: Sculpture, Dallas, Texas

Page 170: Rodeo at Cheyenne Frontier Days, Wyoming

Page 171: Farmers market, Dallas, Texas

Pages 172–173: Cherry blossoms, Washington, D.C.

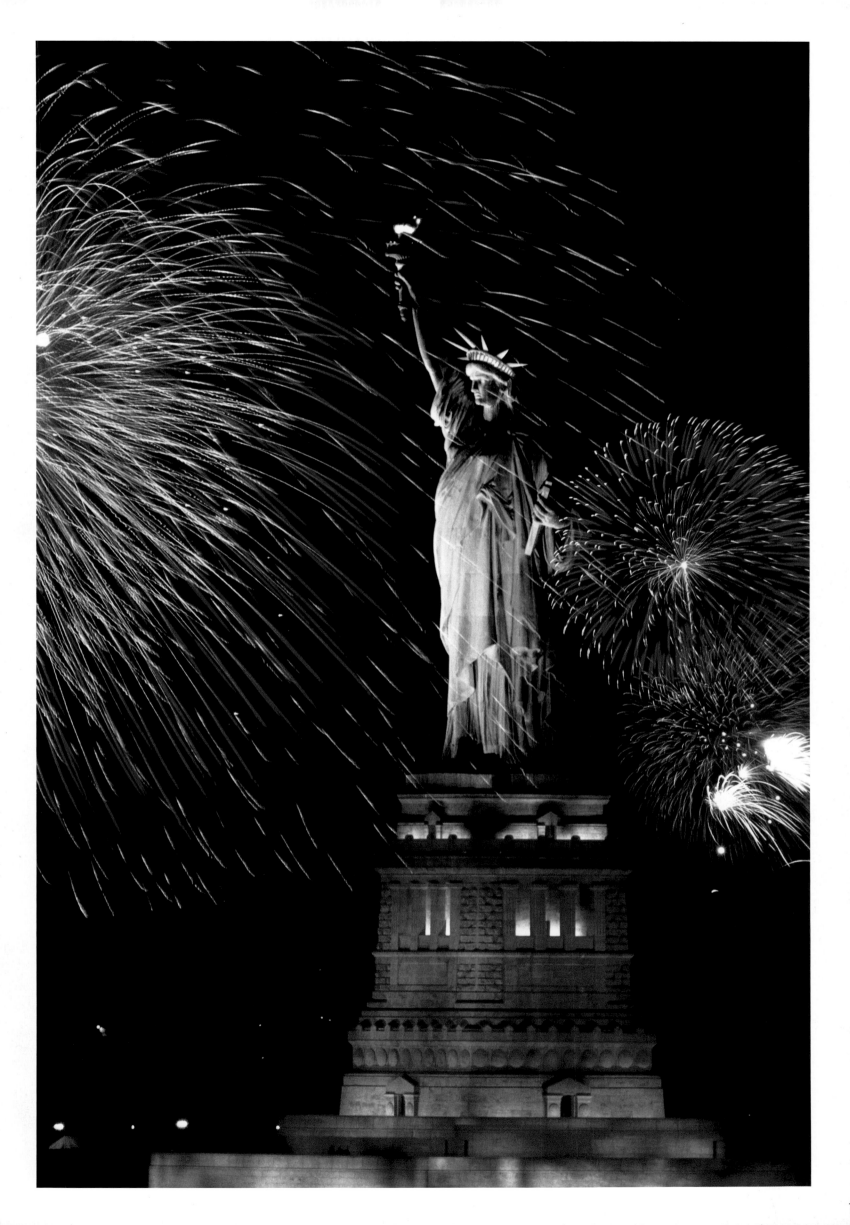

Page 179: Empire State Building, New York, New York

189

ACKNOWLEDGMENTS

Thank you to all the Americans who have smiled and helped me. Pulled me out of sand and out of the ocean, put me in the air, sailed me on the water, and put me on their horses. The American has an open heart, and I'm grateful for that.

Special thanks to:

Alaska: Doug Geeting and Fritz and Anne Iversen

California: Alice Friedman and Sandy Segal

Delaware: Rico Allen, the Olsen family and Gigi Windley

Maryland: Lee Wilson

Montana: Ralph and Candice Miller

New York: Anne for her support, research and love, Bill Black, Bob Ciano, David Frist, Tony Gardner, Jim Good, Gilda Hannah, Nick Iversen, Eddie Millar, Grant Parrish, Joe Pobereskin, Chloe Rajs, Frances Rajs, Janina Rajs, Sam Rosalsky, Jordan Schapps, Jules Solo, Mark Speed, Pete Turner and Jimmy Winstead

Texas: Pete and Dorothy Grant, James Michener, Red McCoombs Ranch and the Y-O Ranch

Virginia: Greg Anderson

Wyoming: Bob and Elaine Walker
the people in the National Parks Service and the many state tourist and motion picture boards

Page 22: "Walking" by Henry David Thoreau, *Atlantic Monthly*, June 1862
Page 72: Speech on agriculture by Daniel Webster, The Boston State House, 1840
Page 106: "The Dry Salvages" (excerpt) by T.S. Eliot from *Four Quartets.* Copyright © 1943 by T.S. Eliot, copyright © 1935, 1936 by Esme Valerie Eliot. Reprinted by permission of Harcourt Brace Jovanovich Inc.
Page 130: "Song of the Open Road" (excerpt) by Walt Whitman, *Leaves of Grass*, 1855
Page 146: Strictly Business by O. Henry, 1910